Beauty of
America

Beauty of
America

Text: Paul M. Lewis
Concept & Design: Robert D. Shangle

First Printing July, 1991
Published by LTA Publishing Company
2735 S.E. Raymond Street, Portland, Oregon 97202
Robert D. Shangle, Publisher

"Learn about America in a beautiful way."

This book features the photography of
James Blank
and Shangle Photographics

Library of Congress Cataloging-in-Publication Data
Lewis, Paul M.
  Beauty of America / text, Paul M. Lewis.
     p.   cm.
   ISBN 1-55988-003-1: $19.95. — ISBN 1-55988-002-3 (pbk.): $9.95
    1. United States — Description and travel — 1981 — Views.
 2. United States — Description and travel — 1981 — Guide-books.
 I. Title.
 E169.04.L48   1989   89-38286
 917.304'928 — dc20   CIP

Copyright © 1989 by LTA Publishing Company, 2735 S.E. Raymond
Street, Portland, Oregon 97202. Litho by Continental
Group Ltd., Indonesia — USA Office: 701 S.E. 97th Avenue,
Vancouver, Washington 98664.

Contents

Introduction

We Americans love to do a little occasional self-puffery, preening ourselves on what we have done as a country and expect to do in the future. A sense of optimism pervades our national consciousness and penetrates the manifold activities that we engage in on a daily basis. Our positive attitudes and expansive nature are inspired in some measure by the bountiful land which sustains us. In these days when the natural arrangement of the world seems in some jeopardy from growing populations and human activities, we have turned more of our attention to the care and preservation of our marvelous corner of it.

Both our material progress as a nation and our optimistic outlook have been fueled by the wealth of our lands and waters. We are beginning to see the wisdom of responsible use of our resources. But beyond the practicality is an emotional attachment to the land that draws upon a long tradition. Many generations have dwelt in this land. Their consciousness and character have always been changed in some degree by the region they called home. The New Englander, tough and resourceful, is following in the tradition of his forbearers, who had to be both innovative and hardworking to gain a livelihood from their land-sea environment. The plainsman, under an endless vault of sky reaching to a horizon that is a remote mystery, puts more of his faith in the Divinity than in the works of man, whose fate seems wholly captive to the whims of weather. The people of the Plains cluster in small towns and medium-sized cities; they are friendly and open, putting great value on personal relationships.

The limitless open reaches of the Southwest seem to nurture another kind of individuality. The Texan is not awed by the vastness of his surroundings, possibly because he is less dependent on what grows on them than is the plainsman to the north. Because much of his wealth comes from beneath the surface, he can confront the more unruly moods of nature with confidence. His glittering cities seem an expression of his assurance that everything is possible.

Those who find their home in the highlands are likely to be of a still different stripe. The Appalachians have their hill people, from north Georgia, through Tennessee, the Carolinas, Virginia, and on up the eastern states, who hold the world more at arm's length than do the people of the piedmont and plains. And he who establishes sanctuary on the slopes of the Rockies or Cascades is just as likely to put a high value on the relative scarcity of other folks in this area.

The lavish variety of landscapes and weather regimes that occur throughout the land has been a strong magnet to settlement. With the comparatively recent enrollment of Alaska and Hawaii on the roster of states, this diversity has become even more emphatic. The nation now reaches north into the Arctic and south into the Tropics. The riches of the earth are expressed in so many different ways in the United States that when a person stops to consider the abundance and variety of it all, he is at a terrible disadvantage. The bounty of natural forms has outstripped the ability of human language to describe it. Some of the more eloquent among us have immortalized parts of it in novels, plays, and poems, but who has been able to encapsulate the cosmic grandeur of the whole country in a work of literature?

This collection of scenes from all of the fifty states of the Union makes no claim to completeness or even to being representative of this or that part of the country. How could it, within the slender confines of one volume? But we do believe that what we have reproduced here is an admirable sample of the immense and ever-changing tableau that is the United States. *Beauty of America* shows us what we have not yet lost, and what, with intelligent concern and perseverance, we will always possess.

— P.M.L.

8

The Valley of Plenty

Until you have seen an Iowa cornfield, stretched farther than the eye can see, you haven't seen a cornfield. But that could be speaking for the whole Mississippi Basin — that enormous piece of real estate lying between the Rockies and Appalachians, running from Canada to the Gulf of Mexico. Food is the thing, from the wheatfields of the Dakotas and the cornfields of Iowa down to the rice paddies and kingdom-sized cattle ranches along the Texas Gulf Coast. The story of the Mississippi watershed is one of cultivation.

Approach Kansas and Nebraska, and the typical comments are made about the endless march of flat fields stretching away from the roadside to the horizon and beyond. For mile upon mile it seems as if the world is, indeed, flat as men used to believe, and covered from edge to edge by a golden carpet of wheat, or endless, uniform rows of corn stalks.

That part of the Midwest that lies on the western slope of the Mississippi basin is called the Plains. The valley of the other side of the big river is also the Midwest, but with a difference. The eastern part is more heavily populated, hillier, and even mountainous, where the Appalachian slopes reach into them. But despite some very large cities in Ohio, Indiana, and Illinois, it still has an essentially rural, open look, with big pastures and grain fields that spread in a checkerboard pattern across a flat or gently rolling land. Its vistas usually betray the hand of man, and textures of his fields dominate the horizon, rather than disappear into it.

The Plains — the real Plains — are another world, different from any other kind of landscape within the United States. They include Iowa, Kansas, Nebraska, North Dakota, South Dakota, and parts of Wyoming,

Colorado, Montana, Minnesota and Missouri. What are the Plains? They're vast empty spaces that may be flat or may be gently undulating, but their overwhelming impact is of space. Someone standing alone under a sky that has no beginning may begin to feel like a fish at the bottom of the sea if he stays there very long. Watching the sun go down on the prairie, the only feature that doesn't go melting off over the far horizon is oneself. Standing there, shorn of pretensions, is an experience that puts new contours into the grooves of memory. The individual consciousness, before the sweep of the boundless prairie, abandons any such arrogant ambition as mastering this land. You don't subdue something that is beyond your conceptual frame. You submit to it, rather.

That is why Plains dwellers, generally, are fatalists. But cheerful fatalists. They seem to value personal relationships more than those whose horizons are more readily definable. Their world is mostly flat and featureless. As far as they can see, everything is more-or-less horizontal, up to a sharply etched horizon that seems to drop off into mystery. Nature is a crushing presence. The sun is a reference point, but the earth flows away under it in all directions, reducing even that bright star to just a lonely glow in the sky that apparently has become lost in a strange universe.

The Plains dweller knows about storms. Violent manifestations from the heavens are expected at some seasons of the year. Weather is both the beauty and the bane of the Midwesterner, the Plainsman, the farmer. The open land offers no protection from the weather in its merciless and savage moods. The storm that brings welcome rain after a long dry spell may exact a payment in the form of a funnel cloud whose terrifying winds destroy everything in its path. Freezing cold and stifling heat visit the Midwest in their turn, but between these extremes, a soft breeze can bring exhilaration to the spirit or soothe away the accumulated heat of a long working day in the fields.

The mystery of the far-reaching plain has never really been solved. The building of the rockies may have had a lot to do with the original conformation of the land that sloped away from the mountains to the ancestral Mississippi. Streams from the Continental Divide spread deep alluvial layers over the land during millions of years. And the glaciers in their periodic visits brought down topsoil that built the wide valley into one of the world's most fertile regions.

Midwesterners have a special feeling for their homeland. Someone who has been there a long time, who is the third or fourth generation of his family in the same place, is likely to believe in his very being that there is no place else to live in the world. The emptiness that brings the sky close to the ground holds no terror for someone who has been partners with it for a lifetime. The spaciousness is friendly to someone who knows that both joy and woe are the lot of those who are subject to its whims. He accepts it, and that way he gains an abiding certainty that he belongs to it, more than he could to any other part of the world. The limitless plains have romance for him. Mountain walls around the perimeter of his sky would give him claustrophobia.

The Tributaries

The "featureless" Plains do have reference points, after all: the great rivers that reach into the interior of the wide basin. The longest, wildest, and probably the most predictable of these lifelines is the Missouri. More than any other river except the Mississippi itself, the Missouri is both the doing and the undoing of millions of square miles of plains. It and its tributaries, such as Nebraska's Platte, are the throbbing nervous system of most of the basin states west of the Mississippi. As befits a river of the Plains, the Missouri starts wandering all over its bed as soon as it gets past the clearly defined banks of headwaters in Montana. The river is still regarded by those who live in its domain as godlike in power, capable of wreaking death and destruction in its demonic moods. Combining with a big tributary like the Republican or Kansas rivers, it has come up with some of the biggest and costliest floods in this country's history. Like the Mississippi, the Missouri was an avenue of steamboat traffic when those romantic carriers were in their heyday.

Bigger even than the Missouri in terms of water volume, the other main tributary of the Mississippi — the Ohio River — rules the eastern slopes of the midcontinental basin. Much of the Ohio River Valley is mountainous, or at least hilly, carrying the westward-reaching foothills of the

Appalachians in eastern Ohio, West Virginia, southern Indiana, and Kentucky. The river has flooded often; in times of heavy rain or melting snow, its 75 tributaries pour a fearsome torrent into the broad waterway. When the volume exceeds the carrying capacity of the river — about once a generation — a flood spreads over the valley, inundating communities along the Ohio's banks. The flooding river, more than any other stream, has been responsible for the Mississippi's memorable rampages, pouring five times as much water into the lower Mississippi as the combined flow of the Missouri and the upper Mississippi.

Western Pennsylvania's Monongahela and Allegheny rivers come together at Pittsburgh to create the Ohio River. The big waterway, coursing through its softly rolling valley, has been compared to Germany's Rhine, from two perspectives: its photogenic valley and its busy barge traffic. The Ohio is one of the world's most heavily used rivers. Its banks are lined with forests and factories, the natural features providing landmarks for river pilots by day, the manmade ones gleaming from the banksides at night.

The Mississippi

The Mississippi — the Father of Waters. Alexis de Toqueville, with his precise French tastes, called the name of the big river an example of the "pompous" Indian language. Maybe. But it is nevertheless apt. Its length — nearly 2,400 miles — and the volume of water it carries put it in the big daddy class. A few rivers of the world, like the Congo and the Amazon, are bigger, or drain even more territory. But none of these other areas can match the Mississippi basin for productivity. The river and its tributaries control the destiny of the vast Midwest and Plains. Each of the five primary tributaries is mightier than most of the country's other rivers. The Missouri, born far over in southwest Montana, is even longer than the parent stream — 2,700 miles. The Ohio River, coming into its big valley on the eastern slope, almost doubles the flow of the Mississippi when the two join at Cairo, Illinois. Three other navigable tributaries — the Illinois, Arkansas and Ouachita — help bring river shipping into the well-watered interior.

The Mississippi begins a hundred miles or so from the Canadian border at two-pronged Lake Itaska, one of Minnesota's 14,000 big and little ponds. The headwaters are not much more than the flow that would come from an open fire hydrant. Summer tourists at the lake do the obligatory "walk across the Mississippi" where the rivulet leaves the lake, either wading or stepping over the 20-foot width on a bridge of rocks. The only boats that can negotiate this stretch of the Mississippi are canoes. The little river is practically invisible as it wanders through the marshy wilds of northern Minnesota for the 40 miles to Bemidji, then turns east and south to begin that long, majestic swing through the heart of the continent and on to the Gulf of Mexico.

The Mississippi is America's trademark. It is the physical feature that identifies this country more truly than any other, being entirely an American river. In its crooked north-south journey, the river becomes many different things as it flows through a number of climates and a variety of landscapes. The headwaters are only a timid little canoe trail, giving no hint of the monster, Olympian river that takes command of the affairs of man and nature in its powerful surge through the whole length of the county. In summer it flows east from Bemidji through a cool, green, lake-splashed wilderness of rice paddies. This is duck country, with migrating mallards and ringnecks congregating where both wild and cultivated rice, and other grains, flourish. The upper river before St. Cloud is also an avenue through some of Minnesota's vast stands of pine. By the time it passes that city and heads for Minneapolis-St. Paul, it has put away its childish belongings and is giving hints as to what it will become as it moves through the heartland.

Below the Twin Cities, beginning at Lake Pepin, the river is encased in the protective sleeve of the Upper Mississippi River Wildlife and Fish Refuge for several hundred miles south to Rock Island. Wildlife flourishes in the marshes and on the river bluffs of this sanctuary. Atop the high banks an observer can take in the sinuous curves of the river, visible upstream and down for some 25 or 30 miles. The Wisconsin hills paint a green and graceful swatch back of the river. Forest, prairie and pastureland combine in a medley of glorious river scenery.

Soon the riches of the upper Midwest begin to find their way to the Mississippi's banks as towns, built on that wealth, line up downriver: Dubuque, Davenport, Moline, Rock Island, Burlington, Fort Madison; plus Keokuk, Nauvoo and Hannibal. The grain of the farmlands of Iowa and Illinois fills the endless parade of barges bound for Gulf ports. The waters of the river are, themselves, a bountiful provider, yielding great quantities of many fish species, including carp and catfish.

It's hard to realize how short a time has passed during the "settling-in" of the river-basin country. The various ethnic strains from the Atlantic seaboard — Germans, Scandinavians, Poles, Irish — started to arrive in force only about a century ago. Through periods of hard times and prosperity, floods, droughts and crop failures, they have stayed and made the Mississippi Valley the guiding star of the world's farmers. But even before western civilization came, when the river and its domain were entirely creatures of the wild, the region was populated by the Plains Indians when the white man began to learn of the great Father of Waters. The Indians are still there, but the river has changed, or been changed, by the spread of an agricultural and industrial society in contrast to a hunting society.

The river's role as a transportation artery becomes apparent as far north as the Twin Cities. At this point the Mississippi is already a big river, now more sedate and business-like after the youthful impetuosity and steep descents of its beginnings in the wet wilderness of forested northern Minnesota. After the Falls of St. Anthony at Minneapolis-St. Paul, the Mississippi is forced into mild behavior by 29 dams and locks strung out all the way to St. Louis. But a big change takes place some miles north of St. Louis. The turbulent Missouri comes in out of the west, practically pushing the main stream aside as it shoulders its way into the channel. For a long while the two rivers keep to their separate channels, the slaty Mississippi following the east bank, the Missouri pouring its turbid stream along the west side. But at Cairo, in the southern corner of Illinois, the giant Ohio adds its tremendous deluge, and from then on the Mississippi takes on its legendary personality. It has become one huge, roiling, tempestuous, muddy shaper of the land. It flows south for another thousand miles in sweeping loops, never staying long in one place, because as soon as it meets an obstacle, it works powerfully to undercut it. Frequently the river has, in flood time especially, abandoned loops by cutting across their narrow base. The new channel then flows by what has become an oxbow, or horseshoe-shaped lake created by the powerful current as it digs itself a new bed. These days such events are not as common because control measures have to some extent diminished the Mississippi's power. But Ol' Man River is still dangerous when aroused. At flood times the bottomland along the path of the lower river is still fair game for inundation, despite levees, dams, or diversion channels.

A large measure of the lower river's scenic quality is contained in the bottomlands, or batturelands, between the river and the levees. A vast hardwood forest of several million acres grows on these lands, providing quickly renewable timber resources for a big world market. The trees are fast-growing, water-tolerant species like cottonwoods, for which a flooding river creates no big problems. On the Mississippi and its tributaries, the cottonwoods of the banksides thrive and grow into a wood that is both light and tough, with few knots. The rich, wet soil provides ideal conditions for the trees, and a forest can be harvested more than once while other trees in other forests have not yet reached maturity. But these great riverside woodlands also protect abundant wildlife, such as wild turkeys and deer, enriching the area in that way, Most of the batture forests are grown on the banks of Arkansas and Mississippi.

Below St. Louis the river drops imperceptibly all the way to the Gulf, and river traffic passes freely up and down without having to resort to locks. The river of history and legend begins to take over as the water rolls by some celebrated riverbank towns: Memphis, Greenville, Vicksburg, Natchez, Baton Rouge. The German and Scandinavian accent grows fainter as English, and then French, influence is revealed in the majority of names. The scenery alternates with high, steep cliffs or bluffs with level forest and meadows.

The antebellum South is still in evidence in some parts of the Southeast, and so, too, in this Mississippi Delta country. Downriver as far as Natchez, in the woods back of the riverside, are some of the extravagant plantation mansions, some quite decayed, some well preserved. Some are deserted, others are lived in, and still others are mere fragments, standing forlorn among the Spanish moss hanging from live oak and cypress trees.

As the river moves from Natchez toward its southern limits, it seems to become more restless still. Channel maintenance and marking become a job requiring unending vigilance and effort. Not only does the channel shift constantly in the powerful currents, but banks get sucked into the stream in places where it hurls itself against the far side of a bend. Channel and bank markers and lights give lots of work to the Coast Guard: the river tends to carry them off and reinstall them at locations of its own choosing. In some things it is still a muscular, muddy mystery, going its own way in spite of most of man's efforts to tame it with the considerable powers at his command.

The river grows wide at Baton Rouge, rolling grandly through a broad valley of farming country until New Orleans. The levees, up to 40 feet high, follow its curving path all the way, for some mighty floods have washed over the lower river delta land. Baton Rouge wears an outer garment of oil refineries and chemical plants, sitting as it does in the center of the rich oil fields of the Gulf region. One of the main concerns now, on this stretch of the Mississippi, is control of the great volume of pollutants that are the inevitable bequest of the widespread industrialization along the river's lower reaches.

A very grand finale, indeed, to the Mississippi's 2,400-mile odyssey is the City of New Orleans. It's not quite the end of the trip, either, because the sea is still a hundred miles away, pushed back by the river's delta building out into the Gulf. But if not a finale, New Orleans is certainly a crowning point. New Orleans is preeminent in human affairs as a city of life, a stimulating place to be. It is one of the country's biggest ports, and one of the lowest-lying ports. The river-bank levees have been built up to such a height that the immense volume of Gulf and river shipping is invisible from town. But it is there, floating on a river whose surface overtops the land.

No matter that, today the Mississippi is hidden behind the levees and wharves of New Orleans. The river is not so wide, as it bends past the

16

Bellingrath Gardens, Alabama

Mount Mc Kinley, Alaska

Grand Canyon, Arizona

Bull Shoals, Arkansas

Carmel Mission, California

Rocky Mountains, Colorado

Mystic Seaport, Connecticut

Trussum Pond, Delaware

Fort Lauderdale, Florida

Stone Mountain, Georgia

Hanauma Bay, Oahu, Hawaii

Sawtooth Mountains, Idaho

New Salem National Historic Site, Illinois

Bridgeton, Indiana

Mississippi River, Dubuque, Iowa

Gage Park, Topeka, Kansas

State Capitol Building, Frankfort, Kentucky

Hodges Gardens, Louisiana

New Harbor, Maine

Drum Point Lighthouse, Maryland

Rockport, Massachusetts

Upper Tahquamenen Falls, Michigan

Upper Gooseberry Falls, Minnesota

"Melrose," Natchez, Mississippi

Alley Spring Grist Mill, Missouri

St. Mary's Lake, Montana

Chimney Rock, Nebraska

Red Rock Canyon, Nevada

Rocky Gorge, New Hampshire

New Jersey

Rockhound State Park, New Mexico

Hudson River, New York

Smokey Mountain National Park, North Carolina
Badlands, North Dakota

Marblehead Lighthouse, Ohio

Red Rock Canyon State Park, Oklahoma

Mount Hood, Oregon

Brady's Lake, Pocono Mountains, Pennsylvania

Newport, Rhode Island

Magnolia Plantation and Gardens, South Carolina
Sylvan Lake, Custer State Park, South Dakota

Botanical Gardens, Memphis, Tennessee

Pecos River, Texas

Virgin River, Utah

Waits River, Vermont

Monticello, Virginia

Mount St. Helens, Washington

Babcock State Park, West Virginia

Burlington, Wisconsin

Grand Tetons, Wyoming

city, as some lesser rivers become when they get near the end of the trail. The Mississippi seems to be returning to its beginnings in its powerful and silt-laden surge past the big port city and on to its rendezvous with the Gulf. It still flows like a river, even though there are only a few more miles to go. No, the mystery is still intact, the muscle is still there as it pours powerfully into the Gulf. The river keeps building more land as if it needs to keep on going, to turn the Gulf into one more riverside lake.

The Glamorous, Golden West

Somewhere out on the Great Plains, Midwest becomes West: you feel it in Wyoming and Montana, and know it for a fact in Texas and Oklahoma. What you feel, and how you know, is difficult to say — the land looks the same, but the sum of dozens of intangibles suddenly adds up to something different than it did in Minneapolis or Des Moines. The land, itself, makes a spectacular commitment to that difference in the form of the Rocky Mountains on its rugged way to the Pacific . . . and beyond, to the western strongholds of Alaska and Hawaii.

The relatively young Rocky Mountain range is scenarist and stage director for the western scenic drama. The Rockies of the United States stretch through Montana, Wyoming, Colorado, New Mexico, and the western tip of Texas to the Mexican border. They dribble over into the neighboring states of Idaho, Utah, and Arizona, where they are known, in part, as the Bitterroots, the Wasatch Range, and the San Francisco Peaks of north-central Arizona.

Apparently the Plains Indians were more or less content to worship the shining Mountains from afar, rarely venturing into their rugged interior. Even the obsessive push of the American pioneers, though it surmounted this barrier, could not really conquer it: this invasion, and the later one of gold and silver miners, affected only the lower fringes of the mountain and forest wilderness. These days some of the range's most spectacular configurations are set aside as preserves, such as those in Glacier, Yellowstone and Rocky Mountain National Parks.

Rivers are the shapers of the earth, even if they all do their jobs a little bit differently. We have seen how the waterways of the Midwest, with their vast water volumes and low gradients, chew away constantly at their banks and pile up great barriers of sediment, wandering erratically over beds as much as 80 miles wide. The western rivers are different. They dig into the earth rather than wander over it (except in flood time). The gentle slope from the High Plains to the Mississippi is not duplicated on the western side of the rockies. Here such fast-moving rivers as the Colorado, the Green, the Rio Grande, the Pecos, the Snake, the Salmon and the Columbia drop down from mountain heights in a frantic rush.

The star of the canyon cutters is the Colorado River. The Colorado's masterwork is so stupendous that it has swallowed up its creator. The Grand Canyon of the Colorado is not quite the world's deepest canyon (Hells Canyon, on the Snake River between Idaho and Oregon, has that distinction), but its extent — about 200 miles — and the intricate carving of multi-hued rock as the river winds along a swift, grinding course over its floor, assures its supremacy as the most spectacular cleft in the earth's surface. The canyon is a monument to the earth's powerful forces, internal and external, acting in conjunction with each other over millions of years. The high Kaibab Plateau, which houses the cutting Colorado, keeps pushing up, now generally more than a mile above the river. Presumably the river will keep cutting down until it reaches its absolute level, and if the plateau keeps rising, who is to say if the Grand Canyon may not, one day, be even grander.

With the Colorado's vast hole on the ground as a superb example, the variety of our scenic West is one of its most noteworthy aspects. Plunging canyons are just as inspiring as high, glaciated mountain ranges. So, too, the "badlands" of the West — the deserts and eroded wastes that cover many square miles in parts of all the states west of the Rockies. The rivers and the winds are the main sculptors responsible for the stark, weirdly sculptured rock formations found in some of the southwest. Utah's Zion and Bryce canyons, and its gigantic, brilliantly colored monoliths carved by the little Virgin river, seems like a series of sculptures that took on a life of their own after they outgrew their creator. Bryce's battalions of colorful limestone and sandstone rock fantasies have a resemblance to a haunted city whose inhabitants are in a state of suspended animation. Arches and Canyonlands, specializing in great, soaring rock bridges and "windows," show the scouring effects of wind and other natural sculptors. Here, too, the Colorado River has been in the canyon-making business, combining with the Green River to chisel deep pathways through Utah's vast limestone plateau.

The biggest desert in the United States spreads over the Great Basin, between the Sierra Nevada and the Wasatch Range. It is not by any means a desert of uniform aspect or climate, including latitudinal ranges and topography that is as varied as a desert can be. The Great Basin deserts are generally high, but include the lowest point in the United States: 280 feet below sea level in Death Valley. California's Mojave Desert is considered closely related, if not actually a section of them. Most of Nevada is included, and parts of Utah, Wyoming, Idaho and Oregon. The other big desert, the Arizona-Sonora, spreads over southern Arizona and into the Mexican state of Sonora. The biggest desert cacti — the Saguaro and Organ Pipe — are almost exclusively limited to this desert.

The western deserts come to an end at a high barrier not far from the edge of the continent: the Cascade Range of the Northwest and the Sierra Nevada of California. These long north-south mountains are among the tallest and most rugged of our ranges. The slopes of the Cascades support vast forests of fir and pine, with lesser stands of spruce and cedar. The Cascades are characterized by distinct peaks, separate volcanic cones that carry gigantic glaciers and tower over the land, their summits sometimes visible for a hundred miles in all directions. Great freestanding mountains like Rainier, Hood and Shasta are not only awesome in bulk and beauty, but also in their ability to create their own weather, as often as not sticking their heads and shoulders into clouds of their own making. They are mountain climber's mountains, offering glacial challenges to all comers. Washington's North Cascades, especially, cluster together in such a wild and rugged jumble of mountains and glaciers that only the hardiest and most resourceful wilderness hikers venture into their primitive interior.

The mighty wall of the Sierra constitutes a more coherent range than the Cascades. Wholly in California, it features several peaks above 14,000 feet, including Mt. Whitney, highest point in the United States outside of Alaska. The Sierra Nevada almost single-handedly makes California what it is and has played an important role in the history of our westward expansion. Donner Pass, the northward crossing of the range, achieved notoriety as the site of the ill-fated winter crossing of the Donner party in the last century. The frantic California gold rush was centered mainly in the western foothills of the Sierra, and many towns today, such as Oroville and Placerville, have names and histories that bear witness to those times. The Sierra's unusual light-colored granite and fantastic glacial scouring have given them some of the most breath-taking rock structures of any mountain system. The valley seems to have been built especially as a seat for the gods.

The coastal mountain ranges, all the way from the Olympics in Washington to the Peninsular ranges of Southern California, present a nearly continuous wall where the continent meets the Pacific Ocean. They are not all lined up at the water's edge. But where they are, as in Oregon and nothern California, the coastal profile becomes a line of sculptured cliffs and headlands of surpassing beauty. In some places enormous, wild promontories reach far out into the Pacific, rising majestically from the foaming waves as if defying them to do their worst. At other places along the coast, the mountains stand back a bit. Here they reach out to the waters with their skirts, so to speak, and the savage ocean has torn at the land to create great perpendicular bluffs, and bays of intricate design. In still other parts of the Pacific shoreline, the mountains have temporarily retired from the coast, and wide, white sandy beaches dip a gentle slope into the welcoming sea.

Farther West

Not very long ago, when people had arrived on the Pacific side after a trip from the East Coast, they could say that they had traveled across the whole country. Nowadays the country reaches much farther to the northwest and the southeast, with Alaska and Hawaii giving the United States a global reach.

Alaska and Hawaii are as wildly different, superficially at least, as anything we have managed to put together in the rest of the country.

Even though the whole of Alaska is certainly not north of the Arctic Circle, enough of it is to make its ice a self-renewing resource. Most of Hawaii — the main island group — is south of the Tropic of Cancer, so it is better at making fire than ice. Everybody knows these days, if they ever thought otherwise, that Alaska is not one big ice field.

Space is, of course, the first thing that comes to mind in regard to what Alaska has. Its 356 million acres come in many forms, and with a variety of weather systems. Alaska has more coastline than all the rest of the United States (10,000 miles in Prince William Sound alone). The Tongass National Forest, on the narrow Panhandle west of Canada, is the largest federal forest in the nation. Alaska's glaciers and ice fields are the largest on earth; anyone who has taken an Inside Passage trip through those fjord-like Panhandle waters, or watched the shoreline of Prince William Sound from the deck of a pleasure cruiser knows how awesome and accessible those glaciers are as they come sliding down to the sea. And Alaska has some close affinities, too, with Hawaii. The weather is quite mild many days of the year — even hot once in a while — in the southeastern and south-central regions. And as Hawaii has some dynamic volcanics, so does Alaska.

Hawaii is tiny by comparison with Alaska: only 6,415-square miles as against 586,400 for the big northland. The Hawaiian Islands have over three times the population of Alaska, however — about 2,000,000. The biggest island, Hawaii, was for a time one of the most thinly populated, but there are indications in the other direction these days. Hilo, the chief city on the island, is growing rapidly after its establishment in recent years as an airline tourist destination. Still and all, each of the seven main inhabited islands — Oahu, Maui, Hawaii, Kauai, Molokai, Niihau and Lanai — has remained relatively unspoiled, with great areas of unaltered tropical beauty.

One obvious reason Hawaii is such an attractive place is the benign climate, freshened constantly by warm trade winds out of the east and northeast. Lowland Hawaii has no winter, or any seasons at all except summer. Honolulu temperatures during the winter months range on the average from 65° to 80°; in summer the lows and highs are in the 70s and

80s. Things are a bit chillier in the more mountainous parts, but except for Maui's Haleakala at 10,000 feet and the 13,000-foot-plus domes of Mauna Loa and Mauna Kea on the Big Island, the high points top off at about 5,000 feet. Some islands and some places on the same island are wetter than others. Kauai's Waialeale peak averages 460 inches of rain a year. Other island locations receive 20 or less. All of the islands get lots of sun; when the rain clouds do come, they do their thing and leave, making way for the sun's rays to bounce off a freshly washed beach or mountain.

Some of the variations among the islands have to do with their relative age. Kauai, one of the oldest, has the softest, greenest landscape. Its long-dormant volcano is clothed in lush foliage, which softens the flanks of its deep, rain-cut gorges. Kauai's famous Na Pali coast is an isolated sanctuary where immense, rugged cliffs plunging into the sea cut off access by land. Oahu, the most populated, has many good swimming beaches. West Mauai, too, has lots of sandy beaches, and the haunting, steep-walled Iao Valley, clothed in green. The Big Island next door has its moonscape volcanic country, but also has vast grasslands and valleys in its interior that contrast sharply with that stark terrain. The waters around the islands are glassy-clear, filled with coral jungles, where skin divers go exploring among the blizzard of fish life that gathers here.

The fascination of Hawaii and Alaska extends beyond the merely physical, of course. Both states, before they became states, were actively involved in American affairs, and have contributed to our history in important ways. Alaska was the goal of hordes of fortune seekers during the Gold Rush, and Hawaii's Lahaina on Maui, in addition to its status as the royal capital of the Hawaiian monarchs, acquired notoriety early as a busy and prosperous whaling port. New England sent both whalers and missionaries to this free-wheeling town.

Whatever course this country takes in the future, it must surely embark on it with greater confidence, now that two invaluable areas of the world have been joined to our western ramparts. Two such glorious accessions need only reasonable care and stewardship from Americans to assure their perpetuation as national treasures.

The East — Mellow and Mountainous

The east is almost a separate civilization from other regions in the country. To some extent this phenomenon has to do with age: just as England and Europe have acquired a certain sophisticated world view that escapes America in general, so the East, with its 200 years on the rest of the country, speaks a language that can be both irksome and instructive to other Americans.

Age is just about all that Easterners can claim in common: the Atlantic Seaboard states admit of very few generalities otherwise. Maine is not much like Massachusetts in either appearance or style; Connecticut, New York and Maryland are not much like each other, or any other place, either; the Old South and the New South exist side by side in places that have had strong local identities for almost 300 years. And southernmost is Florida, where St. Augustine was a going concern of the Spanish some 55 years before the Pilgrim Fathers landed at Plymouth. To a great extent, Florida is a world of its own.

The coastal belt and the states immediately west are, allowing for the coastal plains, wrapped in some of the world's oldest mountains. The soft outlines of their forested slopes suggest ease and stability.

The long Appalachian chain rises in Alabama and Georgia and sweeps north over a wide path, passing deep inland in the area of the southern piedmont. The range turns northeast, bearing nearer the coast of the Middle Atlantic and New England states. Different parts of the Appalachians have their own labels. Tennessee has its Great Smokies and Cumberlands, which extend into eastern Kentucky and southwestern Virginia and West Virginia, reaching up into Pennsylvania to southern

New York and west over to eastern Ohio. The distinctive Blue Ridge Mountains lie east of the Alleghenies and extend from south-central Pennsylvania down to Georgia to Alabama. North into New York and New England are the Catskills, the Berkshires (in Connecticut and New York), the Green Mountains (Vermont), New Hampshire's White Mountains, and the rest of the range on beyond Maine to Quebec's Gaspe Peninsula. New York's tall Adirondacks are a southern extension of a Canadian system.

The high points on these variegated and jumbled mountain systems are not exceedingly lofty — 5,000 and 6,000 feet or so. But many of the individual peaks are quite impressive because they rise as mountain structures from low valleys. New Hampshire's White Mountains have this kind of grandeur, with a dramatic upward sweep that belies their moderate altitudes. Those who are familiar with the Appalachian chain believe it was once possibly as tall or taller than the Alps and the Rockies. And it's also believed that the chain has been worn down by time and ice-age glaciers. Speculations about their former height seem reasonable, in light of the knowledge that these mountains are among the world's oldest. Their age is put at one billion, one million years, or 1,100 million.

The three southernmost states of the eastern region, Alabama, Georgia and Florida, are outside of the Appalachian's domain, except for the northern hills of the first two. Florida may indeed be the flattest big-piece-of-ground in the whole hemisphere, because most of it is at sea level and the highest of its few hills is 345 feet. But the Florida peninsula is really a separate piece of business from the land it is connected with. At one time covered by the seas, it is still in close communion with oceanic waters. Its southern reach, from Lake Okeechobee on down, is wet and swampy, except for a narrow limestone shoreline ridge. Water congregates all over the beautiful north of Florida, too, but there the lakes have a beginning and an end, and the ground is solid enough for a flourishing agriculture. Even though Florida calls itself "The Sunshine State," it receives a great deal of rain to replenish its immense underground limestone reservoirs, those watery places vital to the good health of its rivers, marshes and swamps, such as the Everglades.

One of the truly beautiful mountain groupings in the Appalachian system are the Great Smokies of Tennessee and North Carolina. These densely packed east-west ridges are an exception to the general north-south Appalachian profile. Their other-worldly beauty is preserved in the Great Smoky Mountains National Park. Sugarlands Cove, one of the sheltered valleys in the park, and Greenbriar Cove north of it, are exceptionally well upholstered with such stands of the world's finest hardwood trees. These and other sheltered mountain valleys, with their fertile soils resulting from the mountains' slow attrition, become a wildflower heaven in the springtime. Both the flowers and the trees are remarkable in their variety.

One apparent anomaly of the southern Appalachians is the occurrence, here and there, of a grassy meadow in an ocean of dense forest. Usually found in the saddle between ridges, these openings can be found from Georgia to Virgina. The early mountain settlers in the Blue Ridge valleys used them for pasture lands. This complex relationship with the mountains, involving the use of valley coves and summit grasslands in their daily activities, turned the settlers into a group known as mountain people.

In spite of reliable information to the contrary, westerners are likely to think of the eastern bailiwicks in terms of cities. It comes as a shock to find out that the world's greatest concentration of deciduous broadleaf trees are in the forests of the Appalachians and the mountain borderlands. Add to that the conifers of the northern and southern mountains. The southern pines begin with a dense New Jersey forest belt that keeps going all the way to the piney woods of Georgia and northern Florida, then west to the Mississippi Delta country.

At least one hardwood tree common to Appalachia has a reputation which extends far beyond the eastern United States. That is the sugar maple. It is found in abundance all over the range, from Georgia to Quebec. Vermont has become almost inseparable from the idea of maple syrup. The varied Appalachian forest is put to a variety of uses other than making maple syrup and sugar. White and yellow pines from the north and south make strong building lumber. Some of the most beautiful and rugged woods — maple, black walnut, and cherry — are fashioned into enduring furniture, from cabinets to gunstocks. White oak makes casks, charred on the inside, for holding a distilled product important to the Tennessee economy. The nut trees, as the variety of forest wildlife attests, do a good job of providing for the needs of other species besides the human one.

New Englanders have a reputation for being tough and taciturn, with a dollop of ingenuity added to the mix. It's easy to see how all that developed. The early Pilgrims found the land rocky and unfertile and the winters ferocious. They and those who came after them developed endurance to withstand the climate, and acquired business acumen to make it in a region where farming on a commercial scale was not feasible. The taciturnity probably developed from a necessity to put all their energy into doing instead of talking. The New Englander's sense of self-reliance is an American legend. He got that way by using self-taught skills to prepare himself to make a living, whether by fishing the stormy, marine-rich North Atlantic or by being involved in some kind of manufacturing. Since the beginning, fishing has been of prime importance in New England, where the jagged coastline offers numberless natural harbors. The early settler quickly found great resources in the dense and varied forests of the region's mountains, and handy transportation in the rivers rushing out of those mountains. Ever since they have made use of these resources in connection with their seaports to build up great industries.

As if to compensate for some of the harsher aspects of weather which often visit this part of the county, nature has ornamented inland New England with some of the Appalachians' most gorgeous mountain ranges. The White Mountains of Maine and New Hampshire are among the most impressive heights in the East. Their Presidential Range includes Mt. Washington's 6,288-foot pinnacle, highest in the Northeast. The elevation, the latitude, and the savage North Atlantic have made the tall peak a mountain of storms. It's a great tourist draw in the summer (and very pleasant at that time of year), but snows and high winds keep it closed to visitors from fall through late spring. The glamorous Whites are now, over much of their extent, protected as a natural forest, so that logging activities are controlled. The fact of their preservation, after being long in the hands of private lumber companies, indicates a growing concern on the side of the environment in a part of the country that has many times set an example for the rest of the nation in its emphasis on the values that are important.

The coastal East has a long reach, from north to south and east toward Europe. The New England shore leans so far out into the North Atlantic that it seems, on a map, to be trying to connect up with the Old World again. The New England "tilt" is one of the geographical distinctions of the northeast coast. The marvelously complicated coastal strip of Maine displays a dazzling array of land and sea interrelationships. This "drowned" shore was created many millenia ago when Ice Age glaciers humbled coastal mountain ranges under their tremendous weight, pushing them deeper into the earth. So later on, when the glaciers retreated, the valleys became inlets and fjords and the peaks became islands surrounded by crooked arms of the sea.

To a person only vaguely familiar with the term, "Down East" means anywhere in New England. But the true Yankee narrows the expression to its historical sense, meaning the coast of Maine. Coastal shipping was once said to be headed Down East when traveling north, downwind, along the eastward-turning coast of Maine. It's often a foggy coastline, especially along the part farthest Down East. The fog, which occurs in any season, is caused when two competing ocean streams, the cold Labrador current and the warm Gulf Stream, mix it up somewhere offshore. At such times the dense woodlands, which grow on offshore islands, become even more wild and mysterious. The rocky coastal strip seems to have a "just made" look anyway, enhanced by fog-shrouded mystery. Mt. Desert Island, part of the offshore conglomeration, is a king-size example of these enchanted kingdoms, 12 by 16 miles big. It has thick forest, many lakes, and a range of variety in its plant and bird life that intrigues naturalists year-round.

The lower New England coastal profile sticks a very long nose into the Atlantic at Cape Cod. It actually looks more like an arm, bent at the elbow and making a fist. Whatever shape it's in, Cape Cod gave Massachusetts a 65-mile foot in the ocean. The cape's long outer beach,

76

from the arm's bend to land's end at Race Point, is still about as unspoiled as it was when the glaciers and the ocean put it together, even with the summer multitudes that swarm onto it. Its glittery waters, bright sands, and high-rise dunes are protected in the Cape Cod National Seasore. The upper part of the arm, the east-west portion, has two distinct shores; the northern, "Yankee" one of Cape Cod Bay, where the towns are more austere and the water colder; and the southern shores of Nantucket Sound, where the warmer waters have enticed Bostonians and New Yorkers to establish summer homes. The cape's southern beach is further enhanced as a vacation mecca by the presence in Nantucket Sound of the islands of Nantucket and Martha's Vineyard. These two beautiful pieces of glacial litter have preserved their quiet ways and their old-time charms in the face of increasing attention from the vacation crowds of the Eastern Seaboard. Famed Narragansett Bay, carving up little Rhode Island to the west, has Providence at its head and Newport down by the ocean end, both towns of considerable lustre in a historical and social context.

Long Island Sound comes up next, like a watery underline closing off the New England profile. The Sound introduces the country's biggest city to the Atlantic Ocean, and New Yorkers regard it as their very own sea. Connecticut, comprising the Sound's north shore, also has some claim to it. Long Island, itself, is effectively part of New York City, its western end a distinctive cityscape and the rest of it a suburb, albeit, an attractive one.

The intricate waterfront of New York City's vast harbor is all business, including the Bronx, Manhattan, and Staten Island, although once in a while an isolated patch of open land, almost rural, makes a bright surprise appearance in the midst of countless piers and warehouses and wharf buildings and ships and expressways. North Jersey pokes its intensely industrialized shoreline into this frenetic manufacturing and service complex, too. But other parts of this smallish coastal state dance to a different tune. The South Jersey shore, to cite a notorious example, is beach country with a vengeance, and because of its handy proximity to New York and Philadelphia, both heavily used and heavily publicized. Atlantic City used to be the destination of the summer social set from the big cities. Now the gambling casinos have refurbished its reputation as a place to be. And it doesn't hurt for it to have some of those white-sand beaches strung out for miles and miles along South Jersey's island ramparts. The beaches are still the number-one attraction in the state, outdistancing even oil refineries and gambling as dependable revenue producers.

The Middle Atlantic coast is sidetracked in a large fashion in the New Jersey-Delaware-Maryland-Virginia vicinity by those two estuaries, Chesapeake Bay and Delaware Bay. The bigger by far is the Chesapeake, carving up Maryland good and proper. It reaches up into that state for 200 miles. The bay's convoluted shoreline pinches in to four miles near its head and widens to 40 elsewhere. The Eastern Shore is still relatively unpopulated. Its quiet backwaters are idyllic retreats for man, beast, and fish. The Chesapeake's fishy reputation is no fluke, because it is home to more than 400 species of marine life. Fortunate easterners who live near enough to its shores grow content on the bay's provender.

North Carolina's Outer Banks are a long string of barrier islands that frame her coastline. Some of them are protected by inclusion in the 70-mile long Cape Hatteras National Seashore. The Cape, itself, guards the coast with its tall lighthouse, warning shipping away from the shallows around it. The islands follow the coastline as it swings southwest; they have become seaside resorts after long isolation from the mainland.

The coast's outrigger islands occur in a more-or-less continuous chain all the way from New Jersey to Florida and into the Gulf of Mexico. The sometimes narrow passage between island and mainland is, on occasion, the route of the elusive and eccentric Intracoastal (or Inland) Waterway that wanders along rivers, creeks, bays, estuaries, canals, and swamps, staying just back of the shoreline, except when occasionally forced into open water. Those famous "Golden Isles" of Georgia — Cumberland, St. Simons, and Sapelo among them — form an honor guard for the Waterway. Georgia's offshore treasures, or some of them at least, are surprising examples of the gorgeous coastal wilderness still in existence on the southeastern shoreline. Still farther south, the elusive Florida coast hides behind offshore island beaches nearly all of the 350 miles or more to the tip of the peninsula. A few of these sandspits have been promoted to celebrity status, far beyond what would surely be expected of a sea-girt piece of coral rock or of a limestone ridge covered by an overcoat of white sand. A few of these are Daytona Beach, Cape Canaveral, and Miami Beach.

Broadly speaking, the various wonders of the nation's eastern shores don't end with the Everglades National Park on the point of the Florida Peninsula. The Florida Keys dribble on for another hundred miles. These coral rocks curve in a southwest arc toward the gulf. The clear, shallow waters of the coral reef bordering the Keys are ablaze with color from the living coral and the gaudy marine life that frequents the coral ridges and recesses. The water around the Keys is warm and the beaches are scanty. Off big Key Largo the "beach" is under water in Pennekamp State Park, where skindivers may go exploring.

There's still much more to the Florida coastal story, to be sure. The longer part of the state's shoreline is on the Gulf side, curving north and west up along the Panhandle to Pensacola. Except in the Tampa Bay vicinity, the west side is thinly populated. Its lavish natural gifts include a great abundance of offshore islands and rich estuarine waters, where wildlife, from alligators to egrets, comes into its own. If the country's eastern shoreline must end somewhere, probably Florida's Gulf side, with its miles and miles of pristine coasts, puts a fitting cap on it all.